The Revelation of
Interpretation
Dream
Book

Apostle Latina C. Campbell

ISBN: 978-1-955312-52-3
Printed in the United States of America

Story Corner Publishing Inc.
3801 Indian River Rd. Suite 13031
Chesapeake, VA 23325

Storycornerpublishing@yahoo.com
StoryCornerPublishing.com

Dedication

To every anointed dreaming Joseph that was persecuted and left for dead because no one wanted to believe your dreams!

TABLE OF CONTENTS

Introduction

Have you ever had dreams that were so bizarre that you had to pinch yourself to make sure it was a dream? The dream felt so real that you could smell, taste, touch, or even feel every detail. Dreams are thoughts, images, and sensations occurring in a person's mind during sleep, but most importantly, they are messages from God. God sometimes speaks to us or shows us things in our dreams because we are too busy to hear from Him when we are awake. Sometimes that is the best way for God to reach us with important messages because we have no choice but to pay attention. When God speaks to us, it is considered "prophecy." Prophecy is simply a message from God.

Many tend to put God in a box or think of God in one set way, not realizing that He is powerful and can do anything. In addition to God doing what He pleases when He chooses, God speaks in many ways. He speaks audibly while we are awake, through prayer, scripture, music, clouds, signs, dreams, visions, etc. I want to focus on dreams for the sake of this book.

Acts 2:17 "In the last days, God says,
I will pour out my Spirit on all people.
Your sons and daughters will prophesy,
your young men

will see visions, your old men will dream dreams."

God used dreams in the Bible many times to communicate His will, reveal His plans, and announce future events. However, biblical dream interpretation required careful testing to prove it came from God (Deuteronomy 13). Both Jeremiah and Zechariah warned against relying on dreams to express the revelation of God **(Jeremiah 23:28-32). Dream interpretations and the revelation of a dream are two different things.** Interpretation is the act or way of explaining an explanation. Revelation is to make something known that was previously secret or unknown. Therefore, an interpretation is not the mystery God reveals concerning the dream because God shares revelation. **Dreams are not always what they seem. Consequently, we must pray to God and ask for revelation. God alone reveals the mysteries, interpretation, and revelation of dreams.**

> Genesis 41:16 "I cannot do it," Joseph replied to Pharaoh, "but God will give Pharaoh the answer he desires."

∞∞∞∞∞ ∞∞∞∞∞ ∞∞∞∞∞ ∞∞∞∞∞ ∞∞∞∞∞ ∞∞∞∞∞

> Genesis 40:8 "We both had dreams," they answered, "but there is no one to interpret them." Then Joseph said to them, "Do not interpretations belong to God? Tell me your dreams."

This book reveals the revelation of God concerning topics we have all had questions about at some point in our spiritual journey with God.

Chapter 1

Elevating Your Relationship with God

In this dream, I walked into the bathroom. As I was about to leave, I noticed a creepy face staring at me in the shower. The face looked like a scary muppet. It was big, green, round, and hairy. The eyes were big and bright, with lips that were thick, wide, and black, which stretched from one side of its face to the other. The face startled me because I knew it would not just disappear. At first, I thought my mind was playing tricks on me, but when I realized it was really there, I started praying. I realized it was a demon. I began to bind the demon and commanded it to flee from the bathroom in Jesus' name, but it just smiled at me. I called on Jesus repeatedly to see if that would cause the demon to leave. It then laughed at me hysterically. I got quiet and asked God why the demon did not go and what was so funny.

Something inside of me forced me to say the name Yahweh. I felt as if God consumed me and used my mouth to say that name. As Yahweh flowed out of my mouth, the demon stopped laughing. I called out Yahweh again; then, the demon had a worried look on its face. God then reminded me of when He told my family and me to start calling His son Yeshua instead of Jesus. I screamed out Yeshua, then the demon stepped forward from behind the shower curtain, and I could see its entire body. It had the face and head of a muppet, but horns also appeared on its head. It had the body of a goat. The head was huge and disproportioned from the body because the body was small. I kept calling on Yeshua, and the demon rolled into a ball, shrinking smaller and smaller until it disappeared. I was relieved that the demon was gone. Then I woke up.

Revelation

I remember God leading my family and me to sit in on certain ministry services. I would always ask God why we should sit during other ministry services when we had our own ministry to cultivate. The Lord revealed that we were not sitting under anyone but Him. We had to go on assignment and observe the "do's" and "don'ts" of ministry. God pointed out the things that He was not pleased with and told us not to bring those very things into our ministry. In other words, one could say we were in training to ensure our ministry ran just as God wanted it and not how everyone else was doing things. We must remember when God gives us something such as a vision, ministry, a child, business, etc. that, He holds the blueprint of how it should grow or what it should become. We should always seek the one who holds the vision to ensure everything runs smoothly. There are many traditions but only one God. God also had us attending ministries with different doctrines. One of those ministries wore napkins on their heads and referred to Jesus Christ as Yeshua HaMashiach. It got on my nerves hearing them say Yeshua instead of Jesus, but I asked God the purpose of us being there. At first, I did not know Yeshua was simply Jesus in Hebrew. No one from those ministries made that clear to the newcomers. Once God revealed where the word Yeshua came from, I just figured those people wanted to sound profound and religious because they were not fluent Hebrew speakers.

Therefore, I would never refer to Jesus as Yeshua, although I knew the words were the same. I did not speak Hebrew, so I was not thinking about using words from that language. One night in prayer, the Lord revealed to my husband that He wanted our family to start referring to Jesus as Yeshua. I rejected it because of my thoughts and feelings towards the religious people using the name Yeshua instead of Jesus. I figured that when I prayed, God answered me just the same as when I sealed my prayers with Jesus Christ versus Yeshua

HaMashiach. I continued to close my prayers in Jesus' name.

Once I had the dream where the name Jesus Christ did not work, I began to call out to God in fear. The Lord revealed that I was in disobedience because I refused to elevate in my relationship with Him. He allowed me to squirm a little at first in my dream with the demon to see if I would yield to His request of using the name Yeshua instead of Jesus. I know now that our relationship with God should constantly grow because there are many levels of God. We should not have the same relationship with God as we did when we first met Him. God is very mysterious and infinite in all His ways. God goes on and on forever in all of who He is. Therefore, we should forever learn about who God is, His son, and His Holy Spirit. God is three parts, all wrapped in one. Each piece of Him holds so many details we could never explore in a lifetime.

God was pushing me to grow in my understanding of Him. God wanted me to learn another side of who He is and that He is in all languages because He created them. Sometimes change is scary, but with God, change is necessary. Now I'm not saying that everyone must call His son Yeshua to reach a new level in God, but I am saying that when God pushes you to the next level, go with Him. God will lead you by His Holy Spirit on where to go, how to get there, and when you should arrive. Above all else, go with God!

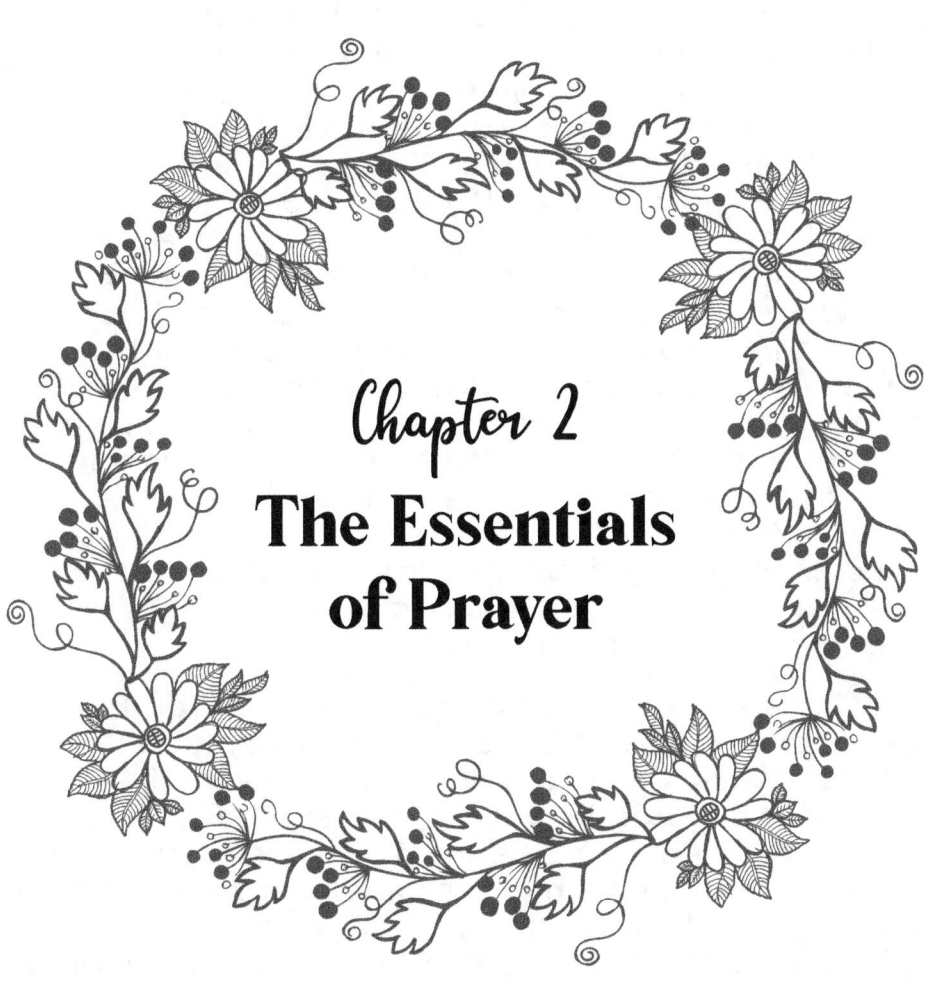

Chapter 2
The Essentials of Prayer

In this particular chapter, I want to outline a couple of dreams that I had referring to prayer and spiritual warfare.

When I married some years ago, I remember having these sexually explicit dreams. The dreams would always be the same, but the people would be different. It would start with a beautiful woman befriending me. She would be super nice and touchy at the same time. Once she won my trust, she would come on to me very flirtatiously. It was almost like she intoxicated me with her touch, eye gestures, and smile. I would fall prey to her desires every time. She would undress me and begin to kiss my body all over. Once she made her way down between my legs, she would use her long tongue to pleasure me until she knew I was ready to melt in her mouth. I was so wrapped up in her that I did not realize she had given a signal to a man to join us. Once he appeared, I was not alarmed because I was open and wanted more. This man would always be naked, abnormally tall, muscular, strong, inviting, and appealing to the eye. He always had a thick, long penis fully erected and ready to penetrate me.

Once the woman finished using her tongue between my legs, she would stand beside me to kiss my lips as the man entered my vagina. At first, he would be gentle with me. After he inserted his entire penis inside me, he would ask me questions as he had his way with me. He would ask, "do you love me? Can I have you to myself? Can you have my baby? Can I marry you?" I would always get stuck in my mind as he asked me the questions repeatedly. I enjoyed the penetration so much that I could not utter any clear words. It was as if my body was numb, and I had no control over it. The weird part was I could only feel sensations of pleasure in my vagina. I could feel all of him, and I wondered how he could put his entire penis inside me. As he penetrated me deeper and deeper, he got louder with his questions. I still could not get out any words, but the thought of my husband would always come to mind at some point. Then I would finally get my words together to tell the man I could not be with him. The man continued asking me the questions ignoring my response for weeks, hoping I had changed my mind. I stayed consistent with my answer. Then the man grew so furious that he evolved taller and stronger before me. Every time I fell asleep then after, He would enter my dream and lock me down with his hands around my neck and continually penetrate me so hard until it felt like I was gushing blood from my vagina as I climaxed. I thought his penis was going to rip me in half. He would rape me until he was ready to explode. I could feel his penis inside of me grow bigger and become so hard that I knew when he was prepared to ejaculate. Before he could even ejaculate inside of me, I would wake up from the dream in fear.

Those sexual dreams felt so real that I woke up in great pain, drenched in sweat, and my underwear soaked in semen. It would even take me some time to get out of bed. It was as if I had sex all night with a hundred men! The angry sexual dreams went on for months. A few months later, I found out I was pregnant! I was so happy and relieved to give my husband the baby he finally wanted. It was his biggest desire when we first married. I was very cautious about everything I did, who touched me, and where I went. The one thing I could not escape was the man waiting for me in my dreams.

When I would go to sleep, he was always there, ready to rape me. These dreams did not include the woman to ease me into being open and ready for him because I made him angry by rejecting his request. He would grab me up by my throat and painfully force his massive penis inside of me. As he thrust deeper inside my vagina, he would scream in my face with great rage. He would rape me repeatedly while ejaculating gallons of semen inside of me as I could not escape it after a while. I would feel it run down my legs in my sleep. The man often said, "I should have had his baby instead of my husband's." He hated the fact that I was pregnant and not with him. He wanted to be my spiritual husband. As the man ejaculated, he hoped to plant another baby inside of me too. Every morning I would wake up in puddles of semen and much pain. Therefore, I knew someone was touching me in my dreams, and I was not delusional. I was afraid to go to sleep after the man raped me the first time, but I could only fight it for so long before my body shut down. The man in my dreams raped me for months until I took a stand with prayer.

Revelation

I remember people talking about having wet dreams, but they would brag about them with great enjoyment. They could not wait to get back to sleep because they were in love with the person having sex with them in their dreams. When I had sexual dreams, I would wake up full of shame, guilt, and regret because I had a new relationship with God, and I was married. I also lived a life of sexual perversion before God saved and delivered me. I thank God for cleaning me up, and I did not want to go back to perversion, even in a dream. When I was single, I would have sexual dreams very seldom. Then they elevated occurring every night after I got married. I would pray and ask God why I had these dreams when I knew my husband was fulfilling me in the bedroom. I got no response from God. I thought maybe we had opened a door or portal once we started having trouble in our marriage. I knew my husband loved me, and I loved him, but everyone and everything was fighting against our marriage. No one wanted to see us happy, and I mean No One. They would try their hardest to turn us against one another, hoping we would divorce so we could be miserable like them.

Once we announced that we were pregnant, all hell broke out around us. People hated that we were happily married and expecting a baby. The enemy was fighting us with everything he had, plus using everyone he could to prey on us. I found myself going to war not only in prayer but fighting in my dreams too. When I realized the man in my dreams was furious after he found out I was pregnant, I knew he was sent to destroy our baby. I began to fast and pray even harder, begging God to tell me who this man was and how to get rid of him. I also started researching demons and discovered that there are demons that visit us in our dreams during the night to have sex with us if we are open to receiving them. The demons would plant demonic seeds destined to steal, kill, and destroy us by any means. My research still did not explain what I was going through in my dreams because it was not just regular sex. I knew there was something more to my dreams but could not pinpoint it. As I continued to pray, I would bind the sexual demons that traveled in the night, but no breakthrough would happen. I would still go to sleep and continuously get raped by the man until, one day, I had a miscarriage. I woke up to real blood and realized it was no longer a dream!

I went to the hospital, and the doctor told my husband and me there was nothing they could do. I had to allow the baby to pass through. I was depressed, stressed, and didn't know what to do. I bled for seven days. I cried out to God, demanding an explanation because He promised me a son. The Lord then revealed that it was Satan in my dreams, appearing as a spiritual husband. Sexual demons appear in dreams to make covenants as "spiritual husbands and wives." Once you have sex with them, the marriage is sealed. In my case, Satan himself was after me, and he wanted me to vow to him verbally. Satan also desired the child I was carrying since I would not give him a child of his own.

The Lord had to step in and take the baby to keep him safe, hence why I had the miscarriage. The baby was too powerful for Satan to get his hands on him. Satan wanted me to fall prey to him in my dreams so he could have free access to the baby. He knew I would not allow him to get next to me while I was awake. I was fully delivered and did not want to turn back to my evil ways with Satan. Therefore, he had to sneak in while I was unaware and sleeping. When I did not say "yes" to him in my dreams, he hated me even more.

God directed me to the scriptures in the twelfth chapter of the Book of Revelations which gives an overview of a pregnant woman in heaven. I had so many questions. The revelation was of Satan turning into a dragon and starting a war in heaven to attempt to take the baby from the womb of the pregnant woman in heaven. God came to her rescue as she gave birth. God took the baby boy into His care and sent the woman into the wilderness He provided for her under His protection and provision. God loved and cared about the woman and the baby. Therefore, He did what was best for them both. I cried when God gave me that revelation because all I could think about was giving my husband the child that he prayed for after we got married. Although God stepped into my situation and took the baby for protection, the miscarriage caused more stress in my marriage. I even contemplated divorce for many months. God told me that He placed my husband and me together for His glory and to let no man, not even us, put asunder what He has joined together. God reminded me that my body is not my own because it belongs to Him first, then my husband. Also, any child that I bear belongs to God as well. That revelation put me at peace, knowing that God had our baby and Satan did not accomplish his mission. I decided to stay with my husband to work out our marriage.

The sexual dreams stopped, so I slept in peace again. Shortly after, I became pregnant again with our second child together. I was afraid that Satan would show up again to make sure I had another miscarriage, but God assured me that I would have the baby no matter what happened. He also told me it would be a boy and to call him Elijah, meaning My God is Yahweh. Elijah was also predestined to work miracles and to stand against the plots of Satan, witches, and demons! He would be able to combat whatever warfare that came his way. Our unborn son, Elijah, would be strong and fully engulfed in the glory of God.

After God spoke these things to me, He took me on a journey of spiritual warfare training. He woke me up every night from 12 midnight to 3:00 am to pray and seek Him for instructions. God revealed mysteries to me on how to win the war against the enemy when he came for my family or me. Sure enough, Satan would try to attack me in my dreams again, but God would step in every time.

Dream #2

I had another dream that I was in a house. The house was unfamiliar and cluttered with furniture, books, and trash, but I began to explore anyway. When I stepped into one of the rooms, I was greeted by an enormous, dark shadow. The shadow overtook me, and I could feel my body levitating off the floor as my back slid up the wall. Then suddenly, I gasped for air as if I could not breathe. I realized that there was a hand wrapped around my neck that was protruding from the shadow. The shadow grew so dark that I could not see in front of my face after a while. I called out to God, asking for help because I knew I could not get rid of the shadow alone. I asked God for the identity of the demon that had me locked against the wall. Then God informed me that I was not dealing with a demon but Satan. It was Satan himself choking me against the wall. God said Satan is not a demon but an angel who has fallen out of His will. I immediately began to beg God to free me of Satan's grip because I knew of the power Satan possessed. God commanded Satan to back off me, and I was released from his hands. I woke up horrified at the fact that Satan was able to get that close to touching me in my dream again.

Revelation

I thought about this dream often. I wondered if I did not have enough breath to call out to God, would Satan be able to kill me in my dream? I am so grateful to have a relationship with God. Throughout getting closer to God, He taught me spiritual warfare. One of the things that I learned was always to call the demon out if I could. I do not know every demon by name, but God does. Therefore, I ask Him to reveal in prayer. I also learned God is the only one powerful enough to destroy the works of darkness, Satan, and demons.

As I began to ask God multiple questions concerning this dream, I wanted to know why Satan was after me again because I was not pregnant at the time. God revealed that I left an opening for Satan to get close to me and into my dreams because I moved out of my prayer position on the wall. God created me as an intercessor that is supposed to be on the wall praying and interceding on behalf of others. For a while, I stopped praying for others because I gave into multiple distractions in my life. For a short period, I even stopped praying for myself and my family. The Lord told me that every time I was out of position off the wall of prayer, Satan had access to reach me again. God invested a lot in me. Therefore, as I pray, it destroys Satan's plans, and he hates me for that. I know now that I have grown strong in prayer, so demons don't have a fighting chance which is why Satan himself will show up for me. I have surpassed certain levels of warfare, and Satan wants me dead because he doesn't want me in his way anymore. I know it is only by the power of God I walk in that holds off Satan. Therefore, I truly give God all the glory because, without Him, I would be dead.

Prayer is essential in our lives because it is our lifeline and communication that we share with our Father, God. Prayer is an intimate communion that we share we Him. He even goes as far to bottle up our tears as unspoken prayers when we cannot get out the words to speak to Him. We grow closer to God every time we pray, and our prayers become more effective because He reveals more to us. When we pray, we follow the example of Yeshua because He always prayed to the Father, God. We also grow in the understanding of God's heart and wisdom. He even trains us on how to overcome Satan's tricks and plans. Ephesians chapter 6 outlines the importance of the Armor of God. As I was going through spiritual warfare training with the Holy Spirit, He reminded me always to put on my armor and pray. In a nutshell, the armor of God all refers back to God because His word surrounds every piece. God is His word. Therefore, we must ensure that everything we do has God at the forefront. We should always clothe ourselves with God and His Word because He is the key to defeating the enemy. He is the power that we need to cover us. In the Book of Job, chapter 41, Job cried out to God, asking why he couldn't destroy a strong demonic spirit named Leviathan. God let Job know that he could not destroy it in his own strength or power. It was a task for God alone, so Job had to move out of the way.

The Armor of God

Ephesians 6:10-20 "Finally, be strong in the Lord and in his mighty power. Put on the full armor of God, so that you can take your stand against the devil's schemes. For our struggle is not against flesh and blood, but against the rulers, against the authorities, against the powers of this dark world and against the spiritual forces of evil in the heavenly realms. Therefore, put on the full armor of God, so that when the day of evil comes, you may be able to stand your ground, and after you have done everything, to stand. Stand firm then, with the belt of truth buckled around your waist, with the breastplate of righteousness in place, and with your feet fitted with the readiness that comes from the gospel of peace. In addition to all this, take up the shield of faith, with which you can extinguish all the flaming arrows of the evil one. Take the helmet of salvation and the sword of the Spirit, which is the word of God. And pray in the Spirit on all occasions with all kinds of prayers and requests. With this in mind, be alert and always keep on praying for all the Lord's people. Pray also for me, that whenever

I speak, words may be given me so that I will fearlessly make known the mystery of the gospel, for which I am an ambassador in chains. Pray that I may declare it fearlessly, as I should."

---

2 Corinthians 10:4-5 "The weapons we fight with are not the weapons of the world. On the contrary, they have divine power to demolish strongholds. We demolish arguments and every pretension that sets itself up against the knowledge of God, and we take captive every thought to make it obedient to Christ."

Belt of truth- Study the word of God and walk in His truth.

Breastplate of Righteousness- Obey God's instructions and walk in His righteousness according to His word.

The Gospel of peace- Stand firm in oneness with the Gospel of Yeshua and live in peace.

The shield of faith- Build your faith with the word of God and ask God to increase it and hold it up.

The helmet of salvation- Fully give your heart, mind, and soul over to the Lord so He can transform you. Set your mind on Yeshua, and do not conform to this world.

The sword of the spirit- This is the word of God that is two-fold. It rescues us from Satan and sanctifies us for change all at the same time.

Pray consistently- Prayer should be our first language because it is our lifeline, communion, and connection to God. It is how we communicate with Him and receive revelation, instructions, directions, etc.

The Lord's Prayer

Matthew 6:9-13 KJV "After this manner therefore pray ye: Our Father which art in heaven, hallowed be thy name. Thy kingdom come, Thy will be done in earth, as it is in heaven. Give us this day our daily bread. And forgive us our debts, as we forgive our debtors. And lead us not into temptation, but deliver us from evil: For thine is the kingdom, and the power, and the glory, forever. Amen."

Chapter 3

This is What Faith Looks Like

In 2017 I gave birth to a beautiful baby boy name Elijah. I went through hell carrying him, delivering him, and even before my husband and I could bring him home. The pregnancy was a rough journey. My gestational sac ruptured at 29 weeks, and the Amniotic fluid began to leak out, causing the baby to have less room to move and breathe. The doctors panicked because 29 weeks was too early to give birth to a healthy baby. They warned me of all the health problems he could have encountered being born prematurely. I was devastated, but I began to pray non-stop until I could see the promise that God had made me in my arms. God promised me a baby boy, and I know with God, all things are possible and perfect. Therefore, my son would be born healthy. I did not accept anything the doctors told me contrary to Elijah being born healthy and perfect. God plugged my sac and replenished the fluids so that Elijah could stay a little longer inside of my womb. I did not deliver Elijah until he was 34 weeks when the doctors decided to induce my labor to avoid possible infection. God performed a miracle right before me and the doctor's faces. The doctors were amazed because they had never heard of a sac rupture closing on its own, let alone refilling itself. When Elijah was born, he had to go to the NICU because the doctor said he was not breathing fully on his own yet. So, they wanted to treat him with a few oxygen cycles until they felt comfortable enough to release him from the hospital. Elijah spent five weeks in the hospital before he was released to come home. The five weeks of running back and forward every day to the hospital wore my husband and me out because we had other children to tend to as well, nor did we live close. We lived in a different state. Most nights, we spent the night at the hospital with Elijah, and we appreciated every moment with him there.

The night before Elijah was discharged from the hospital, my husband and I slept over, and I had a dream. I remember it like it was yesterday. My husband and I were so excited to be able to bring our son home. We could finally get back to our "so-called normal life," which did not include being in the hospital all day. In this dream, I could feel my body shut down as if I was lifeless. I thought it was because I was so tired, but that was not the case. God had entered our hospital room, and I could also see Him in my dream. We have no real idea how powerful God is. Any time He can enter a room in real life and make His presence known in a dream is powerful.

At first, it looked like a bright light, and I did not think anything of it until the light got so bright that I had to close my eyes. If I did not close my eyes, I think I would have probably gone blind. As I closed my eyes in my dream, I could still see the light, only much clearer. The light resembled a very tall figure. It was weird because I had never seen anything like it. When I focused on the light, God began to speak to me. He let me know He was the figure in the room visiting me, and He wanted to touch Elijah. I was afraid to speak and look directly at God, even with my eyes closed. I was in my mind wondering what to do. God himself showed up to give me a message about my marriage and our son. He told me Elijah would be healthy and that he would walk in due time. God also told me that an owl that can't see at night is useless or purposeless. As God spoke to me, the weight of His presence and words weighed me down to the bed so that I could not even move. Once God was done talking to me, He disappeared, and I woke up gasping for air.

Revelation

We never know when or if God will visit us. Scripture tells us that He will appear like a thief in the night. We should always be ready, or shall I say, in right standing with God. I'm happy that God allowed me to live while in His presence and even more filled with joy that He wanted to speak face to face with me. God confirmed that Elijah would be okay because He knew I had some worries about our baby's health. God also knew my husband, and I was under a lot of pressure with all that was going on in our lives then. Therefore, God came to remind me of why He put us together. "An owl that can't see at night is useless" was the quote God left me to ponder on. I had to ask God repeatedly what the interpretation of this quote was. As I sat writing this book, the revelation had become so clear. In my dream, I had to close my eyes to see God. In the scriptures, you will find that without faith, it is impossible to please God. Faith is an unseen thing according to Hebrews 11:1.

Therefore, faith is seeing in the dark or having your eyes closed to what's in front of you. Faith is believing that God exists and He will do what He said He would do. Owls see their best at night because they were designed to see in the dark. Even the dreamer was called to see at night. Not only does the owl see at night, it has 3D vision and can spot things from a far distance. God wants us to walk in faith, the unseen, or the darkness. In the dark place is where God is waiting to lead and guide us because He is the light in any situation. We must depend totally on and trust in Him to get us through. God does not want us to trust in ourselves or other people.

God does not even want us trusting in idols or worshiping other gods because He is the one and only true God. God encouraged me to have faith in knowing that our son Elijah would be healthy and whole. He also wanted me to trust that my marriage would work out no matter what trials or tribulations raised against us. God reminded me that it is possible to see in the dark because He designed an animal such as an owl. God wants us to see 3D spiritually in our dark situation, and the only one we should be focused on is Him.

The biblical story that came to mind was of Daniel. Daniel was sent to the lion's den because he refused to stop praying, going against the king's orders, but he had faith that God would rescue him from his dark situation. The next day Daniel walked out of the lion's den unharmed, and it caused the king that worshipped idols to reverence Daniel's God. God covered Daniel because of his obedience to Him and his faith. Our faith will go through many trials to elevate our relationship with God. Each day we should learn more about God through studying His word to build our faith. Exercising our faith is non-negotiable if we want to please God. He knows the way because He is the way, the truth, and the life. Don't lose faith in God no matter what you see with your eyes open. Just close them and focus on God.

Hebrews 11:1 "Now faith is confidence in what we hope for and assurance about what we do not see."

Romans 10:17 "Consequently, faith comes from hearing the message, and the message is heard through the word about Christ."

Chapter 4
Casting Out Demons

In this dream, I was walking through a transitional house for women. I visited each room to ensure each woman was doing well and getting ready for bed. I walked into one of the rooms and saw one woman hiding in the corner and afraid to look up. She saw me walk in and began to cry out for help. As I entered the room, I noticed a purple hand towel floating in the air. She quickly pointed to the towel and ran past me out of the room. I looked at the towel again, and there were small spots of light forming under the towel. In my head, I asked God to make sense of what I was seeing. I got a little closer to the towel and noticed fingers coming out of the specs of light as if they were portals. The fingers startled me because they were not human fingers. They were green, scaly, alien-like fingers. I stepped back, and my heart began to race because an arm appeared connected to the fingers. Before I could move out of the room, a tall, green, scary monster emerged from the purple hand towel that floated mid-air.

I froze, and I could not move. I asked God to show me what to do, but there was no response. The only thing that popped into my head was The Lord's Prayer. Therefore, I began to recite it, hoping the monster or demon would disappear. As I reached the prayer's end, speaking as quickly as possible, the demon looked at me with a smile. It tilted its head and looked at me as if it wanted to ask, "are you done yet?" I was mortified!!! I thought if I prayed The Lord's Prayer, the demon would be unable to do anything else except leave the room, but I was wrong. God then graced me with enough strength in my feet to start running. I looked back only to see the demon chasing after me down the street. I grew more afraid and then woke up in a cold sweat.

Revelation

Over the years, I attended several deliverance churches where deliverance happened very seldom until there was no evidence. I asked God why there was a lack if there was a great need for people to be set free from bondage. He expressed that in order to be delivered, demons must flee first. I then wondered why the service leaders did not take the time to handle the task. My first thought was maybe it was too hard or took too long. Before my dream, I begged God multiple times to teach me how to cast out a demon so I would not be afraid to walk in the power He gave me. He did not respond to my prayer. Therefore, I began researching different scriptures to understand the basics. I wanted to know if anyone in the Bible days did it and how. I also asked the church leaders, and they all had different responses. None of them gave me a clear-cut answer, as if casting out demons was impossible or a thing of the past. I started to doubt that I had the power to cast out a demon, so I gave up the thoughts.

After this dream, I began crying out to God because I knew this dream symbolized the lack of understanding, power, or anointing I possessed to cast out a demon. My ministry would also involve casting out demons because the Lord showed me I, too, have a deliverance ministry. I am also a believer in Yeshua HaMashiach, better known as Jesus Christ. Yeshua told us we should do greater works than He, and He definitely cast out demons. I asked God how my deliverance ministry would bring Him glory if He had not given me the understanding of how to set His people free.

Finally, God gave me the revelation of my dream, which tied into me casting out a demon or the lack thereof. He said the key to it all is to believe. God asked if I believed what I was praying while casting out the demon. You must walk in the power (Holy Spirit) and authority, knowing you have what it takes to get the job done. Fear and doubt must go. We must be confident in the power of God. We must allow the Holy Spirit to take over entirely because it has nothing to do with us but the power of the Holy Spirit. The Bible says that demons are cast out by the Word of God and by the power of the Holy Spirit. Only born-again Christians have the Word of God and the Holy Spirit in them. Nonbelievers do not have the Word of God or the Holy Spirit in them, and they thus do not have the power or authority from God to be able to cast demons out of anyone. Until you walk in the authority God has given you, without a doubt, you will not be able to cast out a demon.

I have realized over time many leaders walk illegally in God's power pretending to be saved, anointed, live holy, and even possess the power of God altogether. Therefore, true deliverance cannot take place because the Holy Spirit is not present. We alone do not have the ability, but we must have the faith. It is the Holy Spirit within us that gives us the power.

Three Mandatory Factors to Cast Out Demons:

Accept Yeshua/ Jesus into your life to be born-again (saved).

Romans 10:9 NIV "If you declare with your mouth, 'Jesus is Lord,' and believe in your heart that God raised him from the dead, you will be saved."

Acts 19:16 NIV "And the man, in whom was the evil spirit, leaped on them and subdued all of them and overpowered them, so that they fled out of that house naked and wounded."

Acts 19:15 NIV "And the evil spirit answered and said to them, "I recognize Jesus, and I know about Paul, but who are you?"

Acts 19:13 NIV "But also some of the Jewish exorcists, who went from place to place, attempted to name over those who had the evil spirits the name of the Lord Jesus, saying, "I adjure you by Jesus whom Paul preaches."

Luke 10:17 NIV "The seventy returned with joy, saying, "Lord, even the demons are subject to us in Your name."

Must walk in the power of the Holy Spirit by living Holy.

Matthew 10:8 NIV "Heal the sick, raise the dead, cleanse the lepers, cast out demons. Freely you received, freely give."

Matthew 12:28 NIV "But if I cast out demons by the Spirit of God, then the kingdom of God has come upon you."

Luke 11:14 NIV "And He was casting out a demon, and it was mute; when the demon had gone out, the mute man spoke; and the crowds were amazed."

Luke 9:1 NIV "And He called the twelve together, and gave them power and authority over all the demons and to heal diseases."

Mark 1:39 NIV "And He went into their synagogues throughout all Galilee, preaching and casting out the demons."

Mark 6:13 NIV "And they were casting out many demons and were anointing with oil many sick people and healing them."

Matthew 10:1 NIV "Jesus summoned His twelve

disciples and gave them authority over unclean spirits, to cast them out, and to heal every kind of disease and every kind of sickness."

Matthew 8:16 NIV "When evening came, they brought to Him many who were demon-possessed; and He cast out the spirits with a word, and healed all who were ill.

Luke 10:19 NIV "Behold, I have given you authority to tread on serpents and scorpions, and over all the power of the enemy, and nothing will injure you."

Acts 13:3 NIV "Then, when they had fasted and prayed and laid their hands on them, they sent them away."

Believe with confidence that you can cast out demons.

Mark 16:17 NIV "These signs will accompany those who have believed: in My name they will cast out demons, they will speak with new tongues;."

Acts 8:7 NIV "For in the case of many who had unclean spirits, they were coming out of them shouting with a loud voice; and many who had been paralyzed and lame were healed."

Mark 9:29 NIV "And He said to them, "This kind cannot come out by anything but prayer."

Matthew 17:18-21 NIV "And Jesus rebuked him, and the demon came out of him, and the boy was cured at once. Then the disciples came to Jesus privately and said, "Why could we not cast it out?" So Jesus said to them, "Because of your unbelief; for assuredly, I say to you, if you have faith as a mustard seed, you will say to this mountain, 'Move from here to there,' and it will move; and nothing will be impossible for you. However, this kind does not go out except by prayer and fasting."

Luke 9:40 NIV "I begged Your disciples to cast it out, and they could not."

Chapter 5
Call Them
By Name

I had a dream that I walked a guy out to his car, but before we got in, there was a woman who approached us. She started flirting with the guy. He seemed to enjoy her conversation a lot which set off a red flag for me because he was married. As the woman spoke to him, I could see her transforming into something inhuman I had never seen before. I immediately asked God to reveal what I was seeing so I could cast it out because I could see it was a demon. The Lord told me its name was "Lilith." I called the name out loud, and I commanded it to come out of the woman in Yeshua's name. The demon then fell to the ground as if it had lost all its strength, but I could see it slowly turning back into the woman. The guy and I made it to the car, and once we shut the doors, a group of demons surrounded the vehicle so that we could not go anywhere. I began to pray even harder, fighting back fear. As I prayed, I could feel a sense of peace take over my body as if God had shown up to pull me out of the dream. Then I woke up.

Revelation

Once I woke up from the dream, I felt utterly exhausted, but I went into prayer immediately, asking God for revelation, instructions, and interpretation. God revealed I had to call the demon out by name if and when it's given to cast out a demon. One gift of the Holy Spirit is "the gift of identifying spirits." Once you identify the spirit, you won't have to work hard to cast out a demon. The Lord gave me the word "Lilith" after I asked Him to reveal the demon that the woman had transformed into before me. I researched it, and indeed it was the name of a demon. Demons like to stay in hiding so they can remain anonymous. Even Jesus asked the name of the demons that possessed a man. The demons responded, "we are Legion, for we are many." Always remember demons travel impacts like wolves. Therefore, once you cast out one, many others must also come out. Hence, the group of demons surrounded the car in my dream because I only cast out one demon leaving many others behind needing to come out.

> Luke 8:30 NIV "And Jesus asked him, "What is your name?" And he said, "Legion"; for many demons had entered him."

> Matthew 4:10 NIV "Then Jesus said to him, "Go, Satan! For it is written, 'You shall worship the Lord your God, and serve Him only.'"

> 1 Corinthians 12:7-11 NIV "Now to each one the manifestation of the Spirit is given for the common good. To one there is given through the Spirit a message of wisdom, to another a message of knowledge by means of the same Spirit, to another faith by the same Spirit, to another gifts of healing by that one Spirit, to another miraculous powers, to another prophecy, to another distinguishing between spirits, to another speaking in different kinds of tongues, and to still another the interpretation of tongues. All these are the work of one and the same Spirit, and he distributes them to each one, just as he determines."

Chapter 6

Warning Comes
Before
Destructions

I remember having multiple dreams of God warning me of different things. Most of the dreams were terrifying, so I woke up praying that none of the dreams would happen. Some of them did, no matter how hard I prayed. A dream I had when I was younger was of my father dying. I saw the funeral home and him lying in the casket with a black suit, white shirt, and a red tie. I woke up crying so hard that I could not catch my breath. Years later, my dad passed away, and I walked down the aisle in that same funeral home to see him in the casket with the exact outfit that he wore in my dream. My heart was crushed knowing I saw that day before it happened, and I did not take heed to prepare myself.

I had a second dream when I was in high school involving someone I dated, and I thought he loved me until I saw him in my dream with another woman. They were flirting with each other, holding hands, and kissing. The woman told me they were dating, and he was her boyfriend too. I could not believe it, and I began to fight them both in my dream. The dream felt so real that I woke up out of breath, in pain, and feeling like I was having a heart attack! My heart was broken as if I was grieving over a death. My mind wanted to believe it was just a dream, but my heart would not let it go. A month later, I saw the woman from my dream and my boyfriend together sneaking around with each other. By this time, I found out I was pregnant with his baby, and the woman revealed my boyfriend was cheating on me with her the whole time we were together. I was warned in my dream, but I did not want to believe it. Once I saw everything unfold before my eyes, I could not blame anyone but myself because I had the chance to leave after the warning.

In my late twenties I had another dream involving a guy that I had my second child with.

In this dream, he had three car seats in the back seat of his car. One car seat had our unborn daughter in it, another car seat had another baby girl in it, and the third car seat had a baby boy in it. I began to ask his mother questions about the children, and she told me that her son had two other women pregnant at the same time, and I was the third one. She then said we would all have our babies around the same time, and she would have to watch all three. I then saw a fourth woman bring a baby in a car seat to the front door of his house and leave it there in my dream. When I woke up from my dream in the middle of that night, I asked my boyfriend if he had another woman pregnant at that time. He got so afraid that he put his clothes on quickly in silence and left my house. His actions confirmed my dream was a true revelation. I could not understand how I kept picking the wrong guy to have a baby with until God revealed I needed to choose Him first.

After I gave my life to God, I got married to a man He chose for me. I believe my dreams intensified! I began having dreams that were so crazy that I could not explain them to anyone. In one of the dreams, I was walking around in an unusual store. All the shelves were low to the floor. I could stand at one side of the room and see everything with no problem. I then noticed there was a wolf following me, but it behaved like a calm, friendly dog. The wolf even looked more like a dog than a wolf, so I thought maybe it was a crossbreed. It rubbed against my leg and licking my hand, although I did not want it near me because I'm not too fond of dogs. After a while, I figured since the wolf was friendly, it would not hurt me. Therefore, I began to entertain it a little, then it tried to bite my hand. I yelled at the wolf to stop, and it charged at me. I ran behind the counter to safety. Then the animal completely changed into a wild wolf tearing up the store in rage. I woke up and asked God for the revelation. God revealed that the wolf symbolized a woman in my life that I allowed too close to me. She befriended me and was trying to ruin my life, marriage, and children's mind. She was a wolf in sheep's clothing, according to Matthew 7:15. I immediately put up boundaries and have not allowed her back into my inner space. I still pray for her and greet her with love, but that is as far as it goes. I received the warning and took immediate action!

In recent dream, I was working with a group of men. They suggested that we investigated a secret location to complete our assignment. We all gathered at the meeting spot and headed out on foot. We approached a narrow alleyway and had to walk down the path one at a time. At the end was a tall, white, clean, welcoming gate. We pushed the gate, and it opened as if it was waiting for our arrival. As we walked in single-file, I ended up in the back of the line. I was the last to make it through the gates. When I entered, I saw fire everywhere, but it was not hot. The fire only consumed the outer part of the room. I looked down and the floor began to break away from the gate so I could not turn back. I also noticed I was standing on a huge clock with roman numeral numbers and foreign writing on it in the center of the fire. I grew afraid because I was alone and did not know what to do. I was unsure if I should move or stand still. I evaluated the area again to see if there was a way of escape and all I could see beyond the fire was complete darkness. It was so dark that it almost looked as if nothing else was there. I asked God to show me what to do, then I heard a voice. I could not see anyone, but the voice spoke to me and said, "You do not belong here! Go back! This is Hell!" I asked where was my co-workers and the voice said, "You do not belong in Hell! They chose their fate." I blinked my eyes, then I was snatched up and placed on the other side of the white gates in the narrow alley. I walked up and down the alley to see if maybe my co-workers were brought out too, but I was the only one. I began running to my car and woke up. All I could do was cry and worship God for saving me from Hell when I know I mess up daily. I know God could have left me there, but the fact that He didn't, I'm honored to have another chance to get my life in order with Him. I will not allow this warning to pass me by! The scripture that came to mind is "If I ascend into heaven, You are there; If I make my bed in hell, behold, You are there." Psalms 139:8. God showed up for me that time, so I will not abuse His grace.

Revelation

After I started seeing patterns of my dreams come alive, I knew my dreams were real. I could go on and on about many dreams that became a reality. I asked God why He was allowing me to experience these dreams. I thought either it was a test or God was being mean. In most of the dreams that I did not want to see, God was sending me warnings.

Looking back over my dreams, I am grateful that God did show me the warning so that I could be prepared to take the necessary steps. We must realize that God gives us warnings before destruction. Signs could come in any form when dealing with God. For me, He gets my attention in dreams. Before, I did not know I was a dreamer that could hear God's voice, nor did I know God would communicate in dreams. I have discovered many stories in the Bible of people having dreams and visions of God speaking to them. Each time God spoke, it was an important revelation that the person had a charge to do or say something. Our dreams are secrets unfolded before us, so take them seriously. Understand God speaks in any way

He chooses, with dreams being one way. Therefore, I am better equipped to handle the situations I see in my dreams. I thank God for revealing His mysteries to me even as He does with His Prophet. Below are some scriptures involving God's interaction and revelation with man.

> Genesis 40:16-23 NIV "When the chief baker saw that Joseph had given a favorable interpretation, he said to Joseph, "I too had a dream: On my head were three baskets of bread. In the top basket were all kinds of baked goods for Pharaoh, but the birds were eating them out of the basket on my head." "This is what it means," Joseph said. "The three baskets are three days. Within three days, Pharaoh will lift off your head and impale your body on a pole. And the birds will eat away your flesh. "Now, the third day was Pharaoh's birthday, and he gave a feast for all his officials. He lifted up the heads of the chief cupbearer and the chief baker in the presence of his officials: He restored the chief cupbearer to his position, so that he once again put the cup into Pharaoh's hand— but he impaled the chief baker, just as Joseph had said to them in his interpretation. The chief cupbearer, however, did not remember Joseph; he forgot him."

> Genesis 41:25-43 NIV "Then Joseph said to Pharaoh, "The dreams of Pharaoh are one and the same. God has revealed to Pharaoh what he is about to do. The seven good cows are seven years, and the seven good heads of grain are seven years; it is one and the same

dream. The seven lean, ugly cows that came up afterward are seven years, and so are the seven worthless heads of grain scorched by the east wind: They are seven years of famine. "It is just as I said to Pharaoh: God has shown Pharaoh what he is about to do. Seven years of great abundance are coming throughout the land of Egypt, but seven years of famine will follow them. Then all the abundance in Egypt will be forgotten, and the famine will ravage the land. The abundance in the land will not be remembered, because the famine that follows it will be so severe. The reason the dream was given to Pharaoh in two forms is that the matter has been firmly decided by God, and God will do it soon. "And now let Pharaoh look for a discerning and wise man and put him in charge of the land of Egypt. Let Pharaoh appoint commissioners over the land to take a fifth of the harvest of Egypt during the seven years of abundance. They should collect all the food of these good years that are coming and store up the grain under the authority of Pharaoh, to be kept in the cities for food. This food should be held in reserve for the country, to be used during the seven years of famine that will come upon Egypt, so that the country may not be ruined by the famine." The plan seemed good to Pharaoh and to all his officials. So Pharaoh asked them, "Can we find anyone like this man, one in whom is the spirit of God?" Then Pharaoh said to Joseph, "Since God has made all this known to you, there is no one so discerning and wise as you. You shall be in charge of my palace, and all my people are to submit to your orders. Only with respect to the throne will I be greater than you." So Pharaoh said to Joseph, "I hereby put you in charge of the whole land of Egypt." Then Pharaoh took his signet ring from his finger and put it on Joseph's finger. He dressed him in robes of fine linen and put a gold chain around his neck. He had him ride in a chariot as his second-in-command, and people shouted before him, "Make way!" Thus he put him in charge of the whole land of Egypt."

Matthew 2:11-13 NIV "On coming to the house, they saw the child with his mother Mary, and they bowed down and worshiped him. Then they opened their treasures and presented him with gifts of gold, frankincense and myrrh. And having been warned in a dream not to go back to Herod, they returned to their country by another route. When they had gone, an angel of the Lord appeared to Joseph in a dream. "Get up," he said, "take the child and his mother and escape to Egypt. Stay there until I tell you, for Herod is going to search for the child to kill him."

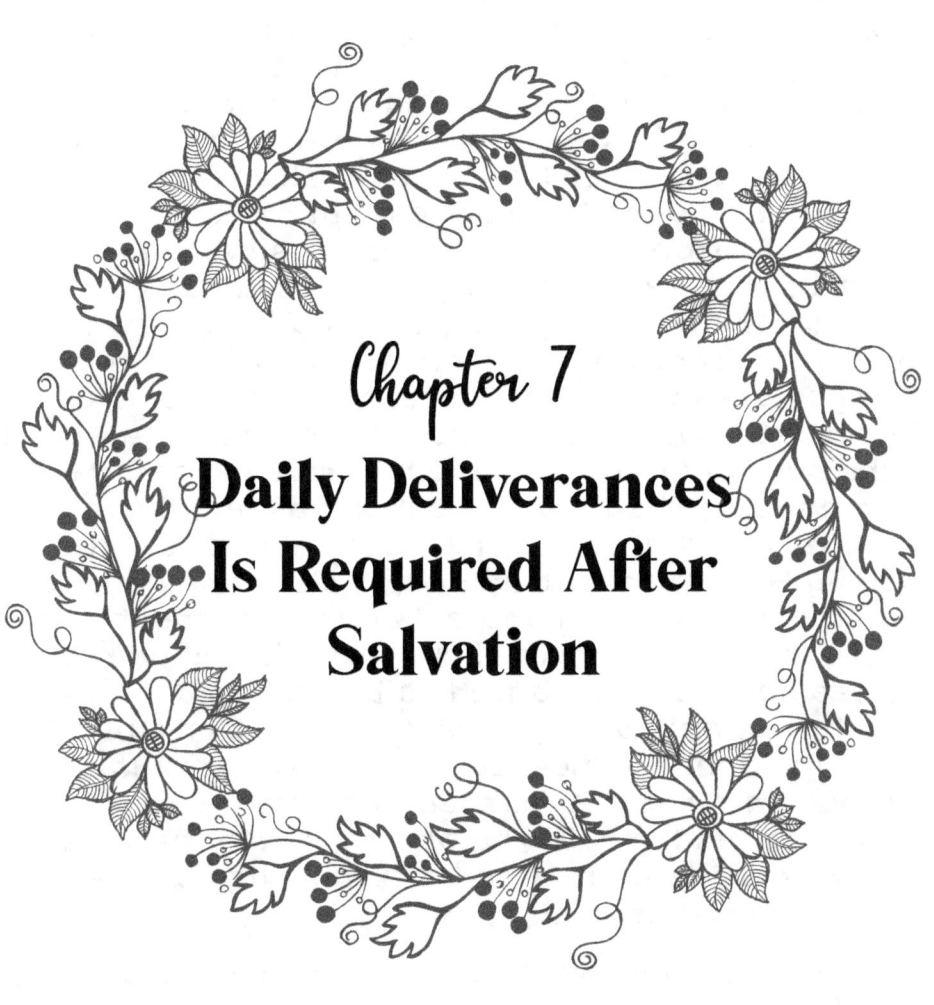

Chapter 7

Daily Deliverances Is Required After Salvation

This dream may be a little controversial for some because many think they can be lukewarm with God and still serve Him with the expectation that God is pleased. This dream displays one of the sinful things I used to deal with, and I am not proud of it. Before I accepted salvation through Yeshua (Jesus), I was endowed with sexual perversion. I prostituted and transitioned to a high-class escort. I watched lots of porn, I masturbated multiple times a day, I slept with many men and women just for fun, and I played with sex toys. After I accepted Yeshua (Jesus) into my life, God cleaned me up and began to deliver me from a list of things considered a sin. Most of the sexual perversion was cleansed off me, but the one thing I kept falling back into was masturbation. All the other sexually immoral things I used to do were pretty easy to let go of, but masturbation would haunt me! The urge would take over my mind, and I would give in for a two-second rush, then I would come crashing down mentally in shame & guilt! I would cry out to God, asking Him to take it away and close the door so I could not open it anymore. I cried out repeatedly, only for God to remain silent. I think God wanted to see how badly I wanted to be delivered. Masturbation was not something I sat around thinking about or needed to do to stay sexually active. I did not get married until after God delivered me from all the other sexually perverted activities. Therefore, I had a steady, healthy sex life with my husband.

I would have never thought masturbation would consume me at a greater level after marriage. I asked God what was going on with me because I knew I could get sex from my husband whenever I wanted it, but it was almost like masturbation would call me louder. I then learned that it was a spiritual battle I was dealing with, so I had to allow God to break it off me. I went through cycles of not masturbating for an extended period, and I would think I was delivered until a sexual thought popped into my mind, then I would masturbate. I realized my prayers were the only thing keeping the demonic spirit of masturbation away from me, but I wanted to be officially delivered. I did not want it to come back and have its way with me again.

I remember one day having a dream after I masturbated and fell asleep. In this dream, I was sitting in a room on the bed, and a huge dark presence opened the door. It was not a shadow, nor was it a person. I knew it was something or someone. Once the door fully opened, I knew it was the presence of God. He walked into the room and flipped over the bed with great anger. Then He walked into another door closing the first door behind Him. Once both doors closed behind Him, I could feel the detachment between God and me. I began to cry, asking God sincerely to forgive me and to give me another chance. In the dream, I could see the sky weeping as the rain poured down heavily onto the glass ceiling above my head. After a while, I saw the door God closed behind Him crack open a little. Then I woke up.

Revelation

> 1 Corinthians 6:19 "Or do you not know that your body is a temple of the Holy Spirit who is in you, whom you have from God, and that you are not your own?

God revealed He walked out of the door on me because I was unclean in His presence due to masturbation. I did not use self-control; instead, I gave in to my fleshly desires every time. He was very unpleased with me. God revealed masturbation disgusted Him because it was sin that contaminated me. God does not want us to do anything He did not create us to do. Everything involving God has a purpose that serves Him. God does not get any glory out of us masturbating because it doesn't produce anything good. It is a gateway that takes us deeper into sexual sin. He did not create us to get a quick fix by pleasing our fleshly desires. When God does something, it is good and does not leave us feeling torn down, shameful, or full of guilt. God's plans push us closer to destiny and purpose. I could not stand before God in prayer or worship with masturbation all over me. Married or single, masturbation is considered sexually immoral, and you will find many scriptures in the Bible warning against such things. God created my spouse to please me sexually, not myself. According to the Bible, God killed a man for ejaculating on the ground instead of placing his seed into the chosen woman.

> Leviticus 15:16-17 "Now if a man has a seminal emission, he shall bathe all his body in water and be unclean until evening. As for any garment or any leather on which there is seminal emission, it shall be washed with water and be unclean until evening."

When we masturbate, we are not following the sexual principles that were put into place in the book of Genesis. Adam and Eve were put together to procreate or multiply and subdue the earth. They were not designed to waste seed or time. Each time we masturbate, seed and time are wasted, no matter how small. Being wasteful does not please God. Many believe masturbation is not a bad thing because it does not involve someone else. Instead, it actually opens doorways for Satan and demons to attach and attack us. The demons can even transfer to our family.

The door reopening at the end of my dream symbolized God's forgiveness and mercy if we genuinely repent. We must have sincere regret or remorse, turn from our sinful ways, and allow God to deliver us. Repentance is necessary, so we can build a relationship with God because it allows Him to change us for the better, which we cannot change ourselves. God loves us very much, and He knows we will mess up hence, why He sent His son Yeshua to die for our sins. Sin separates us from God. Therefore, we must repent daily for the sins we commit. Yeshua's bloodshed enables us to receive forgiveness from God when we mess up. Otherwise, our wage for sin would be death. We must go through daily repentance and deliverance from the sinful things that call our name to enter the Kingdom of God.

Sin: An immoral act considered to be a transgression against divine law.

Romans 6:23 "For the wages of sin is death; but the gift of God is eternal life through Jesus Christ our Lord."

Salvation: deliverance from harm, ruin, & loss; deliverance from sin and its consequences, brought about by faith in Christ.

Romans 10:9 "If you declare with your mouth, "Jesus is Lord," and believe in your heart that God raised him from the dead, you will be saved."

Deliverance: A rescue from bondage or danger.

Psalm 34:17 "When the righteous cry for help, the Lord hears and delivers them out of all their troubles."

Keys to deliverance:

Acknowledgement of sin

Understanding the cross and why Yeshua died

Genuine repentance

Saving faith in Yeshua

Steps to Live Blameless before God:

Be Holy: Live set apart or free from anything contrary to God's Word.

1 Peter 1:14-16 "As obedient children, do not conform to the evil desires you had when you lived in ignorance. But just as he who called you is holy, so be holy in all you do; for it is written: "Be holy, because I am holy."

2 Timothy 1:9 "He has saved us and called us to a holy life—not because of anything we have done but because of his own purpose and grace. This grace was given us in Christ Jesus before the beginning of time,"

Romans 13:13-14 "Let us behave properly as in the day, not in carousing and drunkenness, not in sexual promiscuity and sensuality, not in strife and jealousy. But put on the Lord Jesus Christ, and make no provision for the flesh in regard to its lusts."

Be Perfect: Living God's Word.

Matthew 5:48"Be perfect, therefore, as your heavenly Father is perfect."

2 Timothy 2:22 "Now flee from youthful lusts and pursue righteousness, faith, love and peace, with those who call on the Lord from a pure heart."

Repentance: Ask for forgiveness of sin, then turn away from it back to God.

2 Chronicles 7:14 "If my people, who are called by my name, will humble themselves and pray and seek my face and turn from their wicked ways, then will I hear from heaven and will forgive their sin and will heal their land."

In Conclusion, we must value dreams because they are important messages from God. Dreams are broken into many categories, and we must seek God for revelation. God has many secrets He wants to reveal to us, but we must be still enough to grasp them. Settle your mind and allow God to invade your space. Seek Him in prayer while He is near.

www.ingramcontent.com/pod-product-compliance
Lightning Source LLC
Chambersburg PA
CBHW061325120626
46546CB00007B/2684